This Book Belongs to:

Shelbie Calaman

3 Stories in one

BIBLE HEROES
STORYBOOK

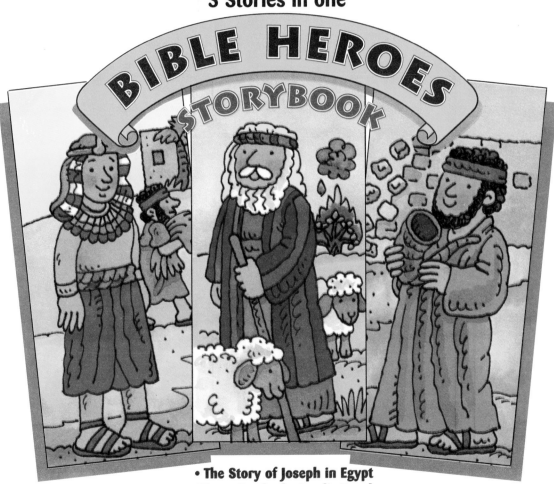

• The Story of Joseph in Egypt
• Moses Leads the Lord's People
• Joshua Leads the Hebrews Against Jericho

THE STORY OF
JOSEPH
in EGYPT

Retold by Andy Rector

Illustrated by Ben Mahan

"This strong young man would make an excellent servant," said the slave trader. "Who would like to buy him?" Soon Joseph found himself walking down the street with a man named Potiphar. "I need you to help feed and clean my animals, Joseph," said Potiphar. "You will help my other servants pick grain in the fields and clean the house. We will take care of you."

As Joseph grew older, he proved to be an excellent servant; Potiphar put him in charge of his whole household. But one day Potiphar's wife got Joseph into trouble and he was sent to prison.

During this time the Pharaoh, who was the king of Egypt, became angry with his cupbearer and his baker. They were sent to the prison where Joseph was. One night the cupbearer and the baker each had bad dreams which they could not understand.

"Tell me about your dreams," said Joseph.

"I saw a vine with three branches of grapes," said the cupbearer. "I squeezed the grapes into a cup I held and a cup the Pharaoh held."

"The three branches," said Joseph, "mean three days.

Pharaoh will restore you as his cupbearer in three days."

Then the baker told Joseph his dream, about some birds eating bread from a basket on his head. " That is not a good dream," said Joseph. "It is a sign of death."

In three days, the cupbearer had his job back with the Pharaoh. And as Joseph had said, the baker soon died.

Two years later, Pharaoh woke up from a disturbing dream that no one—not even his magicians and wise men—could understand.

"Wait," said the cupbearer, "When I was in prison I met a man named Joseph who could understand dreams."

"Get him," said Pharaoh.

Soon Joseph stood before Pharaoh. "In my dream, Joseph, I saw seven healthy cows grazing along the river. Suddenly seven sickly and scrawny cows came out of the river and ate up the seven healthy cows. Can you understand this dream, Joseph?"

"God helps me to understand dreams," said Joseph. "The seven healthy cows mean seven years of a lot of food and grain. The seven sickly cows mean seven years of famine and very little food. Egypt will have seven years of good

crops followed by seven years of famine. You should save some food from the good years and use it during the bad years."

Pharaoh was amazed at Joseph's wisdom. "God has made you wise. I am putting you in charge of my palace, Joseph. No one will have more power in Egypt than you, except for me."

During the following seven years, Joseph had grain stored in barns. After seven years the famine began, but the Egyptians had plenty of food. The Lord watched over Joseph and helped save Egypt from the famine.

MOSES LEADS THE LORD'S PEOPLE

Retold by Andy Rector

Illustrated by Ben Mahan

One day Moses took a flock of sheep on a hillside. He saw a bush that was burning on the hill, but he noticed the leaves and branches did not turn black and crumble to ashes. They remained green and alive. "How strange," thought Moses. "I am going over to get a closer look at this bush."

"Moses! Moses!"

"Who said that?" asked Moses. He heard the voice calling him but did not see anyone else.

"I am God," said a voice from the bush. "The Hebrews are slaves to the Egyptians. They suffer much. You, Moses, are a Hebrew. I want you to go back to Egypt and talk to the Pharaoh. Tell him to free the Hebrews from slavery. I have a new land for them, a land flowing with milk and honey."

One day Moses visited Pharaoh. "The Lord demands that you let his people go or the Nile will turn into blood." Pharaoh refused and so the Nile turned into red blood. The fish died and the air smelled bad.

Moses went to Pharaoh again. "The Lord says you must let his people go or your country will be filled with frogs." When Pharaoh refused, frogs appeared everywhere.

Moses went to Pharaoh again. "The Lord demands that

you let his people go or He will plague your country with gnats." When the Pharaoh refused gnats appeared every-where.

Moses went to Pharaoh again. "The Lord demands that you let his people go or He will plague your country with flies." When Pharaoh refused, flies appeared everywhere.

The Lord continued to plague Egypt. Moses would warn Pharaoh, but Pharaoh's heart remained hardened. The Lord caused the livestock to be sick. He put boils on the Egyptians. He sent a hailstorm that destroyed the crops of the Egyptians. He caused a swarm of locusts to eat what was left of the crops after the hailstorm. He caused darkness to cover the land for three days. Still, Pharaoh would not let the Hebrews leave.

Moses went to Pharaoh again. "The Lord demands that you let his people go or the firstborn son of each Egyptian family will die." Pharaoh refused. At midnight the firstborn son of every Egyptian family died. Even the Pharaoh's son died. He finally decided to let all the Hebrews leave.

The Hebrews quickly left Egypt and headed for the land that God had promised them. Moses led the Hebrew people forward. They came to a sea. "How are we going to get

across the sea?" they cried.

"The Lord is with us," said Moses. He stretched his staff over the waters of the sea. Suddenly the waters divided and formed a pathway of dry land for them to walk to the other side.

Soon the Hebrews reached the other side of the sea. After they were safely across, the wall of water collapsed.

The Hebrews saw the Lord had saved them from the Egyptian Pharaoh. They trusted Moses and sang songs to honor the Lord.

JOSHUA LEADS THE HEBREWS AGAINST JERICHO

Retold by Andy Rector

Illustrated by Ben Mahan

The great leader Moses had led the Lord's people out of Egypt, where they were slaves. These people were known as the Israelites. For forty years after fleeing Egypt, the Israelites wandered in the wilderness looking for the land God had promised them.

Moses, who was by then an old man, died while the people were still wandering. The Lord chose Joshua to lead the people into the promised land. "Be strong, be courageous, Joshua," said the Lord. "The land I promised you is near, but it is full of people who do not believe in me and who will try to destroy you. Believe in me and I will protect you and my people."

Joshua knew his people would have many battles to fight before they found happiness in their new homeland. One day he gathered all the people together. "Do not be afraid of the strange land and the city called Jericho," he told them. "The Lord has given it to us and He will protect us. Remember the promise he gave to Moses long ago."

The Israelites cheered Joshua. "We will be strong and courageous," they cried.

Jericho was a large city surrounded by tall walls and

strong gates. The Israelites had to conquer Jericho if they were to find peace in their promised land.

One day, Joshua sent two spies into Jericho. They went into a house of a woman named Rahab. They hid and rested in Rahab's house for the night.

The king of Jericho knew that the Israelites traveled near his city and he found out about the spies Joshua sent. He sent messengers to the house of Rahab. She covered the spies with stalks of a plant called flax. Then she told the messengers that the spies had already left.

After she closed the door, Rahab ran to where she had hidden the spies. "They're gone!" she said. The spies lifted off the stalks of flax. "Thank you," they said. "You will be kept safe when our people return to take over the city."

To get into the promised land, the Israelites had to cross the Jordan River, which had flooded its banks. "How are we going to get across?" the people asked.

"Trust the Lord," said Joshua. "He will help us enter the promised land." Joshua had some men pick up the Ark of the Covenant—a large gold box that contained the spirit of the Lord. Then they carried the Ark to the bank of the river.

The river stopped flowing and soon, dry land appeared. A path formed where the river had been. The men carrying the Ark walked into the middle of the dry riverbed and stood. All the Israelites crossed the Jordan River.

After everyone had crossed, Joshua said, "Come up out of the Jordan." The men carrying the Ark finished crossing the riverbed to the other side. The Israelites had reached their promised land. Soon the water began to flow again.

Joshua and his army marched around Jericho seven times, as God had instructed. After the seventh time around, Joshua said to the people, "Shout! The Lord is giving you this city!"

The trumpets blared and the people shouted. The walls of Jericho crumbled to the ground.

Joshua said to the two spies, "Quick, go in and get Rahab and her family out of Jericho." The spies rushed in and brought out Rahab and her family. They took Rahab to a safe place, just as they had promised. Soon Israel had control of the city.

The people trusted the Lord and worshiped Him for helping give them the land.